101

EDUCATIONAL

VITO PERRONE

Teaching, Curriculum, and
Learning Environments Chair
at HARVARD UNIVERSITY

CHELSEA HOUSE PUBLISHERS
New York • Philadelphia

CONVERSATIONS
With Your
6th Grader

First Printing

1 3 5 7 9 8 6 4 2

Library of Congress Cataloging-in-Publication Data

Perrone, Vito.
101 educational conversations with your sixth grader / Vito Perrone.
p. cm.—(101 educational conversations to have with your child)
Includes bibliographical references and index.
    ISBN 0-7910-1922-5
        0-7910-1989-6 (pbk.)
1. Education, Elementary—United States—Parent participation. 2. Sixth grade
(Education)—United States. 3. Parent and child—United States. 4. Communication—United States. I. Title. II. Title: One hundred one educational conversations
with your sixth grader. III. Title: One hundred and one educational conversations
with your sixth grader. IV. Series: Perrone, Vito. 101 educational conversations to
have with your child.
LB1048.5.P476 1993   93-16697
649'.68'0973—dc20   CIP

Cover photo: Addie Passen

CONTENTS

Unlike most countries, the United States does not have a formal national curriculum. In theory, each of the 15,000 school districts in the United States creates—with direction from state education agencies—its own curriculum. In practice, however, there are more similarities than differences among these curricula. What amounts to a national curriculum has been created through years of curriculum development by various national organizations related to the various subject areas, through the widespread use of textbooks prepared for a national market, and through standardized testing programs that are national in scope and are designed so that the performance of children in any grade can be compared to the performance of children in the same grade but in a different community or state.

As a result of these standardizing forces, children in North Dakota study much the same subjects in their social studies classes, for example, as students in Massachusetts and Washington. They study their neighborhoods in grades 1 and 2, their cities in grade 3, their states in grade 4, American history in grade 5, some form of world history in grade 6, Latin American and Canadian history in grade 7, American history in grade 8, civics or world history in grade 9, global history or American history in grade 10, American history in grade

11, and either American government and economics or an elective course in American history or world history in grade 12.

The science curriculum becomes somewhat standardized in grade 9 with the study of physical science or earth science. High school students study biology in grade 10, chemistry in grade 11, and either physics or an elective course in biology or physical science in grade 12. In mathematics they study algebra I in grade 9, geometry in grade 10, algebra II in grade 11, and either trigonometry and precalculus or calculus in grade 12.

Each volume in the *101 Educational Conversations You Should Have with Your Child* series contains an outline of the typical curriculum for that particular grade. But you will probably find it helpful to ask your child's teacher about the curriculum for each new grade your child enters. The teacher can give you a fuller account of what is being taught in your school system.

You and Your Child's Education

Welcome to *101 Educational Conversations with Your Sixth Grader*, one of a series of books for parents who wish to be more involved in their children's education. I have written these books with two important goals in mind—first, to give parents a solid basis for talking with their children about their school experiences and thereby gaining further insight into their children's growth as learners; and second, to guide parents toward constructive, education-oriented interaction with teachers and administrators in their children's schools.

In my 30 years of experience in and around schools, I have found that parents are not always clear about what their children are learning in school, about whether their children's overall education is powerful or trivial, challenging or dull. Furthermore, parents often lack a vision of what the schools—at their best—should provide students. We must acknowledge, of course, that not all of what children must ultimately know and understand is learned in the schools. However, the schools do have an intentional curriculum, regardless of the grade level.

In the elementary years, schools expect to teach children reading and writing, as well as certain aspects of science, social studies, and mathematics. They also expect to introduce children to the arts. These efforts should enable children not only to build upon what they learn at home but also to extend their classroom learning into the world outside school. Parents are a vital part of this endeavor. The more you know about the school's intentions and your child's responses, the better for your child's overall education.

Parents invariably ask their children, "What did you learn (or do) at school today?" and are treated to what has become the classic, predictable response: "Nothing." This is clearly a discouraging exchange, leaving parents on the outside or making them feel that they must press their children for details. But a parent's insistence only makes the exchange rather unnatural or even negative, with problematic results. Not only does the parent gain few new insights into the child's education, but the child may come to resent what he or she perceives as a grilling or as a routine, meaningless inquiry. The *101 Educational Conversations You Should Have with Your Child* series is designed to help parents get closer to what their children are learning. It encourages parents to find out what their children understand and also what they do not yet understand. The goal is to make parents' exchanges with their children about school and learning more natural and enjoyable, a mutual treat rather than a mutual burden.

At various times in the school year, parents are invited to parent-teacher conferences, where they often hear a good deal about their children's progress in different subjects. In most cases, however, parents bring too little to these meetings. Rather than being genuine conversations, the conferences are one-sided reports. Parents may leave these sessions satisfied enough, though in my experience few of them say that they are fully engaged by the process. The *101 Educational Conversations You Should Have with Your Child* series should contribute to constructive change. These books are intended to help you inform yourself about what the schools hope to teach and what your children are learning. You should then be able to bring to the parent-teacher conferences some of your own insights and perspectives about your children's educational growth. You will also be able to pose more potent questions to your children's teachers. As a result, your interactions with the teacher should become more interesting and more constructive. The children and the schools will surely benefit.

An important premise of this series is that parents are their children's *first* teachers and their most critically important partners in learning. While this may seem most obvious to parents when their children are in the early primary grades, it is vital for parents to remain involved throughout their children's school lives. This is not, I grant, always easy. For one thing, parents often do not really know what the schools are teaching. In this regard the schools should be expected to provide much better information. Weekly guides would not be too much to expect. Nor would occasional workshops to give parents a fuller understanding of the questions children are asked in school, the books children read, and the principal objectives of the curriculum. If the schools do not deliver this kind of information to parents, then parents should ask, Why not?

Further, while schools typically say they value parent participation, parents are not always treated as full partners. This must change. If the schools do not actively acknowledge and encourage a strong role for parents, then parents themselves should take the initiative. Although this book is most concerned with the parent-child exchange, it will not have succeeded if it does not also empower parents in their relationships with their children's schools and teachers. In the end, the educational partnerships that we so desperately need—between parents and their children and between parents and schools—will be stronger.

101 Educational Conversations with Your Sixth Grader focuses on three areas of interest to parents:

- An overview of the sixth grade, with a look at how classrooms are organized, the kinds of experiences that are offered to children in school, and the basic curriculum—the content of what is taught.

- A collection of conversation starters and suggested activities— a how-to guide for parents who want to explore and expand their children's learning process through creative, stress-free interactions.

- A parent's guide to interacting with teachers and school administrators.

I wish to make one last point in this introduction. In the course of a school year, children study across many fields of inquiry. They read numerous books, view large numbers of films and videos, respond to many hundreds of questions, hear about a myriad of individuals and groups, explore the geography and politics of many countries, and learn many small facts and some larger conceptions. This book, and the others in this series, cannot cover *all* the ground that a child covers in a year. The most it can offer is a variety of useful places to begin. I expect that, once given these important guideposts, parents will be able to develop their own conversations and activities to enhance their understanding of their children's education while in turn enlarging the educational possibilities for the children. I trust that all of you who read this and the other books in the *101 Educational Conversations You Should Have with Your Child* series will have as good a time using the ideas as I have had in putting them together.

1 Your Child's Classroom

The best sixth grade classrooms are *developmentally appropriate*, as are *all* good elementary and middle school classrooms. This means that most activities are based on the physical, intellectual, social, and emotional development of each child, *not* on the children's ages or grade levels. Most sixth grade children, for example, are independent readers; others still need a considerable amount of encouragement to keep reading. The majority of sixth grade children have mastered most basic functions on the computer; others are still tentative. Some are accomplished musicians; others are not yet comfortable with an instrument. Expecting all children to be at the same point, and teaching as if they were, not only limits the learning experience for many children but for some children induces feelings of failure that will not easily be overcome. Attention to individual development rather than emphasis on grade levels is very important. Teachers and schools must, of course, set standards of accomplishment, but they should not expect all children to reach these standards at the same time—or in the same ways.

Developmentally appropriate classrooms are characterized by certain features. Among the most important of these are:

Respect for the Children

- Children's interests are important starting points for learning.

- Children's ideas and work are taken seriously.

- Children are understood to be actively in search of knowledge. Their questions, constructions, and observations are seen as part of the process of building knowledge.

- Children do as much talking as the teachers.

- Children have many opportunities to choose—the literature they read, the projects they do, the activities they participate in.

- Children have *time* to look around, wonder, and dream.

- Children work cooperatively, helping each other.

- Individual, racial, linguistic, and cultural differences are celebrated. They are seen as ways of enriching the children's lives.

Stimulation of Thought, Imagination, and Self-Esteem

- As children move beyond information to understanding, teachers respond to children's ideas and questions in ways that extend their learning rather than encourage rote answers.

- Teachers (and children) ask more open-ended questions than yes-or-no questions. Teachers spark exchanges by saying, "What if we did it this way?" "How else could we do it?" "Who has thought of another way?" "Is there another viewpoint?" "Why was it like that?" "How could it have been different?" "*Should* it have been different?"

- Considerable attention is given to the processes of exploration and discovery, inquiry and investigation.

- Errors are generally seen as steps toward further learning, as particular inventions—not as mistakes or failures. Teachers respond to errors in ways that keep children's self-esteem intact and leave them eager to learn, not fearful of making mistakes.

- Teachers encourage risk taking and provide a safe, supportive environment for it.

An Abundance of Chances To Learn

- All forms of communication are given attention: reading, writing, listening, speaking. The classroom is full of language.

- The classroom is inviting and colorful, with a variety of interesting materials. The children know where these materials are kept and how to use them.

- Sixth grade children's learning activities tend to be based upon textbooks; nonetheless, real experiences, concrete materials, and hands-on activities are also important. Teachers help the children make connections between the various areas of study. To the greatest possible degree, knowledge is presented as an interconnected web, not as a handful of distinct categories that are unrelated to each other.

- Teachers keep learning, and they share what they learn with their students. They demonstrate that learning is a lifelong process and a source of delight.

- Children write their own books, which in turn can be read by others in the class; these writings increasingly reflect children's growing interest in the various subject matter fields, such as geography and science.

- Notes, letters, poems, song lyrics, and all forms of written information and expression are highly visible in the classroom.

- Children read real books by real authors, not just committee-produced "readers" and textbooks.

- Teachers know that learning takes place over time, and that children need numerous and related experiences before they are able to absorb critical concepts and use these concepts effectively as the basis of new learning.

- Interest in literature and social studies grows, matching the earlier interest in science and mathematics.

Opportunities for Self-expression and Connections to the Children's Life Outside School

- Children have frequent opportunities to participate in the creative and expressive arts: music, drawing, storytelling, drama.

- Children have many opportunities to run, climb, and play organized games. Physical activities are seen as important for health as well as for building self-confidence.

- Parents are welcome in the classroom. They are encouraged to be active participants in their children's education.

- Teachers make an effort to connect children's lives in school to experiences outside of school such as reading at home, taking a family vacation, eating a new food for the first time, seeing a movie with their parents, music lessons, organized sports activities, and the like.

Teachers who think in developmental terms understand that they can return often to a particular topic of study. Each time they do so, the children's levels of comprehension will have changed. A child who wants to learn more about Roman mythology, for example, will not be told, "You learned about that last year" or "You'll learn about that when you get to the seventh grade." As much as possible, teachers should allow their presentation of material to be guided by the children's interests, acknowledging that inquiries from students are an important stimulus for learning.

In developmental classrooms, teachers often build the curriculum around themes. For instance, the children may be studying the growth of the city-states in ancient Greece. They will read about the differences between Athens and Sparta, study the relationships of citizens and slaves, come to understand the role of myth in Greek culture, construct models of various forms of Greek columns, recreate ceremonies such as weddings, give reports on the original Olympic Games, perform a Greek tragedy or comedy, do some of Archimedes's science experiments or Eratosthenes's mathematical calculations, look at the sky as Ptolemy did, and draw maps of the world as it was known to the Greeks. Such units of study integrate the children's work across nearly all of the subject areas.

Classroom Organization

Classrooms in the intermediate grades—typically fourth through sixth—often use specialist teachers. Children may spend two or three hours each day with one teacher who works mostly with language arts and social studies, and then they may go to other classrooms for instruction in math, science, physical education, foreign language, and the arts. In such arrangements, children usually study math and science daily (though not always for the same amount of time) and the arts and physical education twice a week.

The specialist teacher arrangement works best when all the teachers involved are members of a team that works consistently with the same children. When this is the case, the teachers can jointly plan the children's work around common themes. The work going on in social studies and literature, for example, can be related to what is being studied in math, science, and music. Moreover, all of the teachers will get to know the children well and can share insights about each child's strengths, questions, and possible problems. Such a team of teachers can provide focused support for each child.

You should know, however, that most schools that use specialist teachers *do not* use *teams* of teachers in this way. Instead, in far too many instances, each teacher functions in isolation, concentrating only on his or her particular subject. Such arrangements promote few, if any, interrelationships among the various subjects. As a result, children's overall learning is less intense; the deep understandings that schools are expected to promote do not emerge as they should.

In other schools, however, children in the intermediate grades continue to be taught in self-contained classrooms, with one teacher all day, every day. In most cases this is more effective than having children work with four or five teachers each day in a curriculum that is not well integrated.

However the classroom is organized, it should support a diversity of uses and contain a wide range of materials. The best classrooms will contain movable tables and chairs that can easily be arranged and rearranged. A box or cubby will be available to store each child's personal belongings; these spaces are treated with great respect by the teachers and the children.

While teachers will organize their classrooms according to their own preferences, the arrangements described below are not uncommon in fourth through sixth grade classrooms.

PRINT MATERIALS AND EQUIPMENT

Many books and magazines related to the various subject fields are freely available to the children. Reading materials will change frequently to accommodate the special topics being studied. (The classroom's collection of reading material includes books, reports, poems, and narratives written by the children; keeping alive a strong sense of authorship is important throughout the intermediate years.) Beyond the classroom collection, the children are encouraged to make frequent use of the school's main library as well as the local public library for special research work and for access to a larger array of biographies and interesting fiction.

Equipment related to the entire spectrum of communications and problem solving is present: computers and at least one printer, a video monitor and tapes, audiotape recorders, drawing boards, and a considerable amount of scientific equipment—microscopes, magnets, pulleys, scales, motors. Children should also have access to easels and paints, a potter's wheel and clay, and musical instruments. (Most intermediate classrooms do not have easels. In fact, in most schools easels begin to disappear from classrooms soon after kindergarten. This is unfortunate. In the best settings, children continue to paint throughout the intermediate years. If your sixth grade child is not still painting, ask his or her teacher why.)

From the fourth grade on, children typically use textbooks in all the subject areas they are studying. These texts try to be comprehensive, which generally means that they cover a great deal of material—probably too much. And they are most often accompanied by numerous peripheral materials, including workbooks. But one major difficulty with these textbooks is that they appear to be so comprehensive that they often become virtually the sole basis for study in whatever subject area they cover: math, science, social studies, or literature. This inhibits teachers from guiding children toward a diversity of study materials and prevents children from forming a broader, more inclusive approach to learning. When reading and subject matter study are confined to textbooks, content is often covered too quickly and too superficially.

Standardized textbooks encourage a passive orientation to learning that should be resisted by teachers and parents, who need to insist to their school boards that textbooks, if used, be regarded as one among many resources, not as the sole resource. Moreover, textbooks are generally written in a bland and colorless style that does little to make a child get excited about reading them.

All classrooms—whether self-contained rooms where the children study all subject areas or rooms designed to serve as study sites for a particular subject area—should be rich environments with a wide range of learning materials. The teachers will consider it important that the children know what materials are available, where they are stored, and how to use them. By this point in their school lives, the children have learned how to use the tools and equipment safely, and they have virtually complete access to all materials. Teachers know that if children do not know what is available to them, or if they must ask permission to use the items (which usually involves waiting), they may lose interest, and their opportunities for exploration will be limited. It should be noted, too, that children in such classrooms do things for themselves: they mix paints and clean brushes, and they operate video systems, tape recorders, and computers. These simple tasks are part of the process of learning self-reliance and responsibility.

Sixth grade children should be well established as creators of material that is seen not only in their own classrooms but throughout their schools. Their writings can be found in the classroom library and perhaps the school library as well; their historical time lines and geological charts are displayed on the walls of the classroom and the hallways; and their models of geometric shapes and of the solar system hang from the ceilings. In some schools each grade or classroom is put in charge of decorating a particular display window or bulletin board in the school's public areas; these cooperative efforts give the children a valuable opportunity to share their work.

MIDDLE SCHOOL OR JUNIOR HIGH SCHOOL?

A final point about school organizations—and one that may affect your sixth grade child—concerns the trend toward middle schools and away from junior high schools.

In many school districts, sixth graders are now being grouped with seventh and eighth graders in what are called middle schools (unlike the traditional junior high school, which included the seventh, eighth, and ninth grades). I approve of this trend. The middle school serves a constructive purpose, acknowledging that in terms of their physical and cognitive development sixth graders have more in common with seventh graders than with fifth graders.

In terms of the philosophy of teaching and the learning environment, however, the best middle schools have more in common with elementary schools than is generally the case with the junior high schools they are replacing. Both teaching and learning in middle schools tend to be more personal and more active than in junior highs; middle schools also place more emphasis on a well-integrated curriculum, with continuity across all study areas. In these respects, in particular, middle schools are more like an extension of the elementary school experience than a junior version of high school.

2 *What Parents Want To Know*

Parents of children in the intermediate grades often ask how large or small the class should be. Parents have an intuitive sense that the class should be small during the earliest years of school, from kindergarten through third grade. But class size is also very important throughout the intermediate and middle school grades. Ideally, a sixth grade classroom should have fewer than 25 children. Class size should be designed to allow plenty of individual attention. The more attention the teacher can give to each child, and the more experiences the teacher can help each child have, the better. As class size goes beyond 25 students, the potential for individual interaction decreases considerably.

In the previous chapter, I explained the importance of having an abundance of varied learning materials in the classroom. My experience is that as class size goes beyond 25 children—which is too often the norm—the classroom becomes a less rich environment for each child. Teachers and parents need to become much more vocal about the importance of class size in these intermediate and middle school years.

Another question that comes up often is, How much homework is reasonable for sixth grade children? Homework is commonly assigned by teachers in the intermediate grades. While some teachers believe that homework is unnecessary—in other words, that the school day is long enough for a child to do everything that needs to be done—I believe homework can be useful, especially if it is interesting, if it goes beyond the daily school activities, and if it is aimed at deepening the child's understanding of what is being studied. A good homework assignment, prompted by a powerful question, might ask the student to interpret, synthesize, or reconstruct an idea or problem.

Homework assignments in the sixth grade might include: Read the new story you wrote to your mother or father. Read for 40 minutes on your own. Think about words related to totalitarianism or social justice. Write an essay about the role of women in ancient Greece or Greek-style architecture in your community. Watch a particular documentary on television and be prepared to tell the other students what you found most interesting or convincing in the program. Scan the editorial page of your local newspaper and note the themes: economic issues, personalities, world events. Or design and carry out an experiment using batteries and circuits.

A sixth grader might also be expected to complete some mathematics problems or begin studying the moon. But sixth grade children should *not* have homework that regularly takes more than an hour and a half to complete. If their homework assignments regularly exceed this limit, parents should inquire about it. And if there is *no* homework, that too warrants an inquiry.

I am often asked about the use of computers in the schools. Many children today use computers at home at age five or six, and a growing number of schools have installed computers in primary-grade classrooms. Much can be done with computers, especially in word processing, mathematics, model building, and problem-solving exercises. And some of the programs now available give children access to large museums and artistic collections as well as to various archives of documents. In addition, some video games emphasize problem solving and could be used in the classroom. By sixth grade, children should be far along in their ability to use the computer for a variety of purposes. Parents should be attuned to their children's level of knowledge and skill regarding computers. If your sixth grade child is *not* a confident computer user, you should talk with his or her teacher.

Parents of intermediate-age children often ask about foreign-language study. Some schools—and the numbers are still very small—begin foreign languages in the early primary grades, often in two-way bilingual programs. In such programs, half the children might be Spanish speaking, for example, and the other half speak no Spanish. Each group learns the other's language.

In most schools that offer foreign language study for elementary students, however, such study usually begins in the intermediate grades. The United States is far behind most other industrialized countries in second-language programs. *All* schools should offer a second language at the intermediate level, if not before. Studying a second language not only provides valuable insights into another culture and enriches the child's world but also greatly strengthens the child's understanding of his or her native language. Parents can and should do more to make sure that their children's schools understand the importance of foreign-language programs.

Sixth grade children are typically engaged in activities outside of school, such as field trips to museums, nature preserves, planetariums, craft centers, businesses, and service organizations.

Some parents question the purpose of such activities and wonder what their children are learning from them; in addition, parents may be concerned that the children are missing the "real" education that should be taking place in the classroom by visiting a museum when they should be having math class. It is clear, however, that field trips *do* enhance classroom learning. A field trip to a museum or factory can make real and concrete what is being studied in the classroom—it is one thing to read about ancient Egyptian civilization, for example, and quite another to get a firsthand look at massive stone structures engraved with hieroglyphs, or to examine three-thousand-year-old mummies and burial masks. In fact, rather than worrying about *too much* out-of-classroom activity, parents should be concerned if their children seem to spend virtually all of every school day within the confines of the classroom.

A Parent's Guide to Teachers' Terminology

As they become involved with their children's schools, parents will hear teachers use many special terms to describe what happens in the classroom. Some of the most important terms are explained below.

LEARNING STYLES

Children learn in many different ways, although each child has a preference for one or two particular ways of learning. These preferences are called *learning styles*. Some children learn most easily when ideas, concepts, and information are first presented visually, through pictures or videos. Others gain understanding only after firsthand work such as writing, experimenting, problem solving, or playacting. Some children need to have ideas presented in a very precise and sequential order; for others, close attention to sequence complicates learning rather than promoting it. Teachers are most effective when they know children well enough to understand their individual learning styles. This lets them individualize each child's learning experiences.

BASAL TEXTS

Basal texts are textbooks designed to provide all students with a common base of information and generally proceed from easier to more difficult ideas. They are available in all subjects and are generally accompanied by numerous prepackaged materials, including workbooks. In the primary grades basal texts are used mainly for reading and language arts, but in the intermediate years they tend to be used for all subject areas. Whatever the grade or subject, though, if basal texts are rigidly followed, they do not match the principles of developmentally appropriate classrooms, and they limit what is learned.

The basal text assumes, for example, that all children of the same age start from the same point. This is especially the case with the language arts texts, but it is true as well of the textbooks in math, science, and social studies. Because everything in these programs is sequential, those who begin the program with less language experience, prior knowledge, or confidence tend to stay behind. Children do not need this kind of negative experience with learning.

LITERATURE-BASED READING PROGRAMS

Literature-based reading programs, often called "whole language programs," take a different approach to reading and the language arts than do the basal texts. In a literature-based program, children read works by identified authors—books and stories such as Madeleine L'Engle's *A Wrinkle in Time*, Charles Dickens's *Oliver Twist*, Amy Tan's *The Moon Lady*, Anne Frank's *The Diary of a Young Girl*, and Mark Twain's *Huckleberry Finn*. They also read primary sources—published diaries, letters, journals, and official records—as part of their study of history. A classroom using this approach to reading will contain many books, both fiction and nonfiction, on a variety of topics and at many levels of complexity. Some of these books will be relatively easy to read, others more difficult. The children make choices about which books they read. A growing number of teachers believe that literature-based programs are not only more appropriate developmentally than skill-based basal programs but help the children become more effective as readers and writers.

DISCOVERY LEARNING

In classrooms organized around discovery learning, children are encouraged to ask questions, investigate subjects that interest them, and find solutions to problems. Teachers tend not to provide answers but rather to help children seek their own answers. Teachers encourage questions by raising questions themselves, by filling the classrooms with interesting materials, and by drawing upon many of the children's own experiences.

For example, suppose that a child is interested in learning how the pyramids of Egypt were built. The teacher might ask the child what ideas he or she already has about how they were built and where more information might be found. The teacher would also suggest additional avenues for exploration. The conversation might go like this:

TEACHER: How could you find out more about the construction of the pyramids?

CHILD: I could check out a book on pyramids, look in the encyclopedia, or call the science museum.

TEACHER: I read an interesting article about the pyramids in the science section of the *New York Times* in the past week or so. It had many new thoughts about them. Possibly the librarian can help you find it. How do you think they were built?

CHILD: They must have used slave labor—people to cut the stones and put them on top of each other.

TEACHER: Are you sure it was slave labor? And how do you think the stones were shaped and moved?

Here is another example of the kind of exchange that is heard in discovery-based classrooms. It comes from a classroom in which the children were studying the moon.

CHILD: Why are there so many sayings, songs, and stories about the moon?

TEACHER: What are some of the examples you are thinking about?

CHILD: The man in the moon, the cow jumped over the moon, blue moon, harvest moon. And all the scary stories about witches and vampires.

TEACHER: Why do *you* think the moon shows up in so many stories and sayings?

CHILD: Maybe because the moon is so common. Everybody in the whole world can see it.

TEACHER: Why don't you ask others to help you make as big a list as possible of all the stories, songs, and phrases about the moon. Then you can see if there are any themes that appear over and over again.

The teacher's role in the discovery-based classroom is to help children find many of their own solutions by giving them a framework for asking and answering questions. Essentially, the teacher introduces children to additional ways of thinking and solving problems.

COOPERATIVE LEARNING

Cooperative learning is a means of helping children work together in order to increase their learning. Cooperative-learning groups are organized to allow students to work on projects together, solve mathematics and science problems, do experiments, share stories, read to each other, and the like. Groups of three or four children working together are particularly effective. In such groups the children will take turns being the moderator, the recorder/reporter, or the monitor of the group's progress.

BALANCE

Teachers throughout the elementary grades, especially those who lean toward developmentally appropriate teaching, talk a good deal about the need for balance. Balance means quiet times followed by active times followed by quiet times; times when children work alone and times when they work with others; times to explore and times to consolidate learning. It is best when the days are varied.

ASSESSMENT

Assessment refers to determinations about children's progress. More and more educational professionals, at least those involved in elementary education, recommend that we stop relying on traditional standardized tests, which typically evaluate children on the basis of fixed standards of skill, achievement, or intelligence and often contribute to misjudgments about children's learning.

The current trend in the lower grades of elementary school is away from standardized testing. I do not recommend the use of standardized tests before grade 4, but even in the intermediate and middle school grades their benefits are uncertain, especially if they are used to make judgments about individual children. Instead of using externally developed, standardized tests, teachers can more appropriately assess students by keeping ongoing records of their performance, documenting students' work on a day-by-day basis. Teachers also keep portfolios of children's work; these are available for the children as well as their parents to review. You will find your child's actual performance in ongoing instructional activities far more informative than the results of any standardized test. Teachers also guide children in systematic and regular self-evaluation. This is especially important. By asking, for example, "Do you feel that you understood what we talked about in science today? Do you think you could explain it to a friend? What do you think was most difficult?" teachers encourage children to define their own learning processes and help them set goals.

COMMUNITY SERVICE

Service learning has become increasingly common in the schools, particularly in the upper intermediate grades and beyond. This aspect of education attempts to help students make connections with the communities in which they live. Sixth graders are often expected to give two to five hours a month to community service activities, such as tutoring or reading to younger children, visiting senior citizen centers or nursing homes, caring for playgrounds, tending gardens that provide vegetables for homeless shelters, and the like. Parents can encourage their children to become involved in community service by setting an example of their own participation, or at least by showing interest in and respect for the child's contributions.

THE TEACHER AS FACILITATOR

A facilitator is someone who makes it easier for another to do something. Teachers who guide, question, and support children in their learning are facilitators; they make it easier for children to learn, giving the central role in the learning process to the children themselves. Teachers who see themselves as facilitators stimulate children and challenge them to think and question. They provide a diversity of materials and activities, and they search for new books and questions that will extend children's learning and enlarge their awareness. They spend much of their time supporting children's investigations. In contrast, teachers who "give answers" most of the time and who do most of the talking in the classroom are not facilitators. In the end, they limit learning.

3 *Your Child's School Day*

What is your child's school day like? In the primary grades—at least through grade 3, and particularly in classrooms organized around the principles of developmental learning—the school day tends to be rather fluid. In these early grades there are few hard-and-fast demarcations between subject areas.

But in the intermediate grades the various subjects tend to be more defined, and the day becomes somewhat more structured. The use of specialist teachers for some subjects adds further structure to the daily schedule in schools that follow this practice. In too many cases the daily schedule in grade 6 is rigidly fixed and compartmentalized—although it would be better if the school day retained more of the fluid, integrated character of the earlier grades. I have been in many classrooms in which students must, because of the need to follow rigid time schedules, set aside work that interests them intensely, such as writing a poem or doing a science experiment, in order to move on to the next subject on the schedule. Arbitrary stopping and starting of this nature does not contribute to the growth of a healthy attention span, and it certainly does not lead to work students can honor, work they see as the *best* they can do.

THE MORNING

Typically the first half hour of the school day (from 8:30 to 9:00 A.M.) is devoted to opening activities: announcements, discussions of special events, the sharing of a poem that someone in the class enjoys or has recently written, possibly a song, and reminders about what needs to be accomplished during the day. This opening session is a way of bringing everyone together; it both creates a transition from the previous day and builds a strong feeling of community in the classroom.

On at least three days each week, language arts and social studies are the focus during the course of the morning (between 9:00 A.M. and noon). This might mean half an hour devoted to uninterrupted sustained silent reading, when everyone—including the teacher—reads, followed by an hour-long writing workshop in which the children work on fiction and nonfiction narratives, poems, and biographies. During the latter period the children will typically read their work aloud to others for response, rework what they have done, and have individual and small-group conferences with the teacher. The teacher will often do some minilessons during this time—for example, demonstrating the appropriate places to use an exclamation point, a semicolon, a colon; pointing out some new and interesting words or metaphors being used by members of the class; or helping the children understand how and when to use different verb tenses.

Social studies is the focus during the 40 minutes or so before lunch. Much of the activity takes place in cooperative groups. Further, it will be reasonably well connected to the language arts activities. For example, the books that the children read during the morning's silent reading period and the stories or essays they write in the writing workshop are likely to involve a subject that will be discussed in social studies.

Two mornings a week the children focus on music, a foreign language, or physical education, for approximately 35 minutes each. Physical education throughout the intermediate grades is generally concerned with movement and running. The children play a variety of ball games, and they may dance or do movement exercises. (If they have music and foreign language in the morning, they will have physical education sometime in the afternoon, and vice versa.)

THE AFTERNOON

At least three afternoons each week, the period from 12:30 to 2:30 P.M. is devoted to mathematics and science. Often this instruction is provided by specialist teachers.

The children spend the final period of the day (2:30 to 3:15 P.M.) with their primary teacher, who is usually the person with whom they spent the morning. During this end-of-day session the teacher reads to the children, often from a classic book that is related to the diverse cultural traditions of the students, such as Lorraine Hansberry's *Raisin in the Sun*, Richard Adams's *Watership Down*, Edith Hamilton's *Mythology*, or Mildred Taylor's *Roll of Thunder, Hear My Cry*. A book like this might take several days or weeks to complete; this extended reading provides a thread of continuity and reinforces the children's sustained concentration skills.

The late afternoon is also devoted to clarifying homework assignments and to journal writing. Students' entries in their journals might center around such questions as "What did I do today in math? In science? What did I learn that was important? What wasn't clear to me? What don't I understand?" Such self-evaluation at the completion of each school day is important. It teaches children to turn their growing analytical and reflective skills upon themselves, and it gives them a feeling of participation, ownership, and control over their own education that will become increasingly important as they advance through school.

4 *What Your Child Learns in School*

This chapter is an overview of the typical curriculum for the sixth grade. It is intended to give you an idea of what your child is learning in school. But because children learn in different ways and at different rates, not all children will grasp a particular part of the curriculum at the same time. While most children will master the typical sixth grade curriculum outlined below, others will need more time to solidify their understanding of some subjects. Teachers and parents who understand development, who do not view the curriculum in terms of rigid grades or steps, will accept this as quite normal.

Even as I outline sixth grade content, keep in mind that some elements from the previous year's curriculum are carried into the sixth grade; such overlap is both common and helpful. And while I have divided the curriculum into different subject areas for convenience, in reality the boundaries between subject areas may not always be so clearly drawn. In fact, the learning environment is better when the demarcations between subjects are not sharp and students are encouraged to focus on the connections, rather than the distinctions, in a body of knowledge. Unfortunately, subject matter delineations take hold in a big way in too many intermediate and middle school classrooms. Social studies suddenly becomes separate from reading, math from science, and so on. It would benefit sixth grade children if this trend were reversed.

Parents should also be aware that while teaching in the first few grades is more informal than formal, formality and structure increase in and after the fourth grade. Even in the intermediate years, however, children's learning requires concreteness and active experiences. In the best sixth grade classrooms, children continue to learn through activities and concrete experiences as well as through the teacher imparting information and interpreting ideas and concepts.

One last point needs to be made about the curriculum. I have refrained from listing all of the *specific* elements that make up the various curriculum areas: the math facts that are learned, the books that are read, the historical figures who are presented. Teachers must introduce children at every grade level to a diverse and rich array of literature and to the many people who make up the traditions of their communities and of the country; at the same time, they must involve children in the fullest use of mathematics, science, and the like. The curriculum should always be expansive, never limiting. A good curriculum is flexible, so that the teacher can easily add not only new subject matter but new levels of complexity. The teacher's main responsibility throughout elementary school is to ensure that children maintain a sense of curiosity, that they love reading and writing, and that they take an ongoing interest in the world around them. The teacher's job is to help children become and remain active and confident learners. That is more important than any particular set of facts.

In doing this job, teachers will probably use a good deal of traditional children's literature. But they will also find that songs or stories from their students' cultural heritages have considerable potential to stimulate children's language development and expand their learning. Similarly, the traditional heroes and narratives of U.S. history will surely emerge in the classroom. But knowing that the traditional histories often excluded women and persons of color, teachers will take care to expose the children to other, less traditional heroes and narratives. And by using math in many different ways and contexts, children gain control of the rules governing addition, subtraction, multiplication, and division. They also come to understand the patterns and relationships by which numbers are governed, as well as to see the uses of math beyond school.

The curriculum throughout the intermediate grades should be rich and full of diverse starting points so that each child—with his or her individual interests, learning styles, and level of development—can enter fully into the learning process. The material being studied should never be so narrowly focused that there is no room for children to pursue some aspect of what interests them most. Suppose a class is studying the topic "extending the voting franchise to women," for example. Some children might want to examine the history of the women's suffrage movement, especially in the 19th century, possibly including Europe as well as the United States in their study. Others might want to give more attention to individual leaders of the American movement such as Susan B. Anthony and Elizabeth Cady Stanton. Some children might focus on how the voting franchise helped create other opportunities for women. And still others might want to write profiles of women who hold elected offices today. The

curriculum must be flexible enough to accommodate all these interests, and it must give the children opportunities to share their dis-
coveries with one another. Above all, the curriculum must always be
intellectually challenging.

As I noted in the introduction, teachers should be expected to have
clear goals for the children they teach. They should be able to explain
what the children will understand, or be able to do, by the end of the
school year, and how everything they do in the classroom is related
to those goals. Teachers should also be able to explain how they assess
each child's progress toward those goals and how they will stay in
touch with parents.

The Sixth Grade Curriculum

Most children entering the sixth grade are reasonably confident
readers and writers. They are generally able to read a wide range of
books, allowing the teacher to present them with an ever-growing
diversity of reading and learning experiences. Moreover, sixth grade
children are able to read for information as well as for enjoyment.
As readers, they find a world of learning open to them.

Sixth grade children will also understand the patterns of mathematical relationships and will be able to use math for a variety of
purposes; will know how to approach science questions and set up
experiments; will be careful observers of the natural environment;
will understand the importance of good health; will understand
history as a human story; will appreciate the interdependency of
people in their communities and across the nation and the world; will
see themselves and their families as producers and consumers;

will comprehend geographical relationships such as direction and geographical concepts such as place, elevation, latitude, and longitude; will enjoy the arts and recognize their place in society; and will see themselves as creators in various art forms. Most important, it is hoped that sixth grade children will continue to be curious about the world, will be confident that they can learn and be filled with the desire to do so, and will be optimistic. Parents can play a large role in keeping their children's curiosity alive by communicating their own sense of lively curiosity about the world. Parents can also help young students maintain an optimistic attitude toward school by making sure that their children understand that there are no limits on their learning or their hopes.

Beginning in the fourth grade and continuing throughout the intermediate and middle school years, children experience a rapid widening of their horizons. They are aware of more of the world, and more is expected of them both at home and at school. During this time it is important that children's confidence be maintained— that they *not* come to say about the work in school, "It's too hard," or "I'm not good at math and science," or "I can't do it." Teachers may be principally responsible for motivating and supporting children at school, but parents must take special care to do the same thing at home.

LANGUAGE ARTS: READING, WRITING, AND SPEAKING

As children enter the sixth grade, most are capable enough as readers and writers, and they have also learned to use spoken language successfully. As I pointed out earlier, they are able to use books both for enjoyment and as useful sources of information. They also know how to use a library and are comfortable doing so. They use writing for a variety of purposes; they understand the writing process, including the value of responses from their peers and revisions; and they have a good sense of authorship. They can also use spoken language effectively in a variety of settings—in discussions, oral reports, plays, explanations, and the like. They understand that language can be used in many different ways.

Where reading is concerned, the teacher's main task in grade 6 is to *keep* children reading. This means continually enlarging classroom libraries, making extensive use of school and community libraries, referring the children to new books, talking about books, reading to the children from increasingly complex works, and working with librarians and other teachers to organize such events as schoolwide book fairs and author visits for the children.

While some schools have organized the language arts curriculum around world literature in the sixth grade, most teachers believe it is more important to keep children reading many different kinds of literature, as their interests guide them, than to concentrate exclusively on a particular country, genre, or period. Regardless of the geographic focus, if any, the study of literature may be organized around themes. Mythology is a popular theme in sixth grade classrooms. When reading is organized around this theme, for example, students will read various cultures' creation stories. They will consider the moral dilemmas presented in such mythological tales as, for instance, the Prometheus story. The students will be asked to compare and contrast elements of the various accounts they read, to explain similarities and differences across cultures and over time, and to give their own definitions of such concepts as fear and courage, right and wrong. They will also write their own myths and moral tales. But even in classrooms that use this thematic approach to literature, the teacher's attitude toward reading should be inclusive, rather than narrowly limiting. Children need to know that when they become readers, a very large world is available to them. In the best settings, teachers will do everything they can to help children step into that large world—and stay in it.

Writing is closely related to reading. Teachers should make sure that children write every day and that they see themselves as active communicators: writers of journals and letters, authors of poetry, biography, and fiction. Teachers know that writing improves with practice and that writing and thinking are closely intertwined, so they hold daily writing workshops—periods when children write, revise, and discuss their work. In some schools teachers say that there is not enough time for daily writing workshops. There has to be time!

Sixth graders should be able to define good writing and to identify the strengths and weaknesses in their own writing and that of others. Writing portfolios that contain files of children's past writing, recently completed works, and writing in progress are well established by the sixth grade. Viewing this work over time is important to a child's self-evaluation and growth; in addition, the portfolio helps the teacher determine what kind of guidance and assistance each child needs. For instance, a teacher might notice that a child consistently confuses "there" and "their," still seems tentative about apostrophes, or is shy about using robust adjectives. These observations would form the basis of focused instruction for that pupil.

Because teachers know that autobiographical and reflective writing is a good means of reinforcing the writing-thinking connection, children are encouraged to keep journals in which they record questions and insights about the various subjects they study as well as personal reflections. Teachers also understand that such reflective writing is another means of promoting self-assessment, an important part of ongoing learning.

Children will know how to use most of the common writing conventions, including punctuation marks, paragraphing, and verb tenses. They will also know how to write dialogues, explanations, and comparisons, although they may not be equally skilled in all of these types of writing. They should, however, be reasonably familiar with narrative, descriptive writing, explanatory exposition, persuasive writing, business writing, and letters to friends. And they will have opportunities to use all of these forms of writing.

The oral aspects of language—especially effective speaking—are always important. Teachers view both speaking and listening as closely related to reading and writing. Children are given many opportunities to speak in a variety of contexts: telling and retelling stories, participating in focused discussions about particular topics, sharing information with other children, giving formal speeches, appearing in plays and readers' theater, assuming the roles of historical figures to gain greater understanding of the lives of others, and reading published poems or their own writings aloud.

Children are also encouraged to examine how language is used in the home, the neighborhood, and the media and to develop an understanding of the power of the spoken word. It would be good if all children became anthropologists of language, observing the various ways that different people use words to say hello or good-bye, to name things, and to express emotions such as joy and anger. Children should develop an appreciation of dialects and of cultural differences in language use; this will help make them aware of the diversity and flexibility of language.

MATHEMATICS

In the sixth grade, mathematics continues to be something that is *used,* something children see as extending far beyond school; unless this is the case, math loses its power to engage the children's interest. While teachers expect children to be reasonably adept with computational skills such as multiplication and division, they are more concerned with whether children understand *when* to add and subtract, to use a calculator, to estimate, and to arrange information on a graph. Sixth grade students typically begin to have an understanding of probability, are able to note relationships among numbers, patterns, or events, and are comfortable with various models for problem solving.

Teachers spend a good deal of time helping the children develop mental models—that is, teaching the children how to visualize problems and solutions. They will also continue to ask the children to develop personal theories by thinking about different ways to solve mathematical problems. Because children of this age cannot fully understand math if it stands on its own, apart from all other subjects, math will continue to be used in social studies, science, and language arts work.

Sixth grade children are encouraged to think out ways to solve problems—teachers often ask, "How can we solve this problem?" For example, the teacher might present the following problem: "How would we go about measuring the area of these shapes?" Or

"If your kite got stuck on the roof of the school, how would you know how long a ladder you would need to get it down?" The emphasis is less on finding the correct answer than on showing that there are multiple ways of approaching the problem. Teachers will provide children with many different problem-solving strategies.

You will probably not see a great difference between the math your child studied in the fifth grade and the math he or she studies in the sixth grade. But you will notice more elements of geometry (especially in the study of shapes) and of algebra (in problems such as $3x + 6 = 15$).

The goal of mathematics in the sixth grade is to help children maintain a good sense of what numbers mean; children should regard math as commonplace, as accessible as any other subject in school. All children, girls and boys alike, should know that mathematics is *not* a mystery that only a select few can master. It should be—and in the best settings it is—fully available to all.

SCIENCE AND HEALTH

Children's interest in science often seems to decline in grade 4 and after. This happens, in part, because science study is too often textbook-driven, passive, formal, and narrow in its scope. But the major goal of science study in these grades should be to keep children interested in science and cause them to believe that they can be successful science students. Positive attitudes about science—from teachers and parents as well as students—are vital.

Children must see and recognize "science" all around them in their everyday lives. Basic scientific principles are at work whenever a child rides a bicycle, puts air in the bike's tires and oils the moving parts, runs, throws a ball, gets water from a well or a faucet, uses a flashlight, takes pictures with a camera, flies a kite, or notices changes in the weather, the shape of the moon, or the visibility of objects seen in daylight or at night. And science is also a basis for understanding what is happening when a child watches cloud formations change or planes move across the sky, plants a garden or trims bushes, reads newspaper headlines about drought and ecosystem damage, or sees the effects of aging or infirmity in others. Good teachers draw heavily on such examples of "science in the world." They ask often, "What do you think is going on?" "Why is that happening?"

Nature studies, the basis of science study during the early years of school, continue during the intermediate years. In the sixth grade, however, physical science, life science, and technology come in for an increasing share of attention. Environmental issues—the definition of an ecosystem, for example—will be prominent in the science curriculum. Beyond learning about and examining machines of all kinds, including computers and mass communication systems, children will also investigate the ways technology affects our lives. In the process, they will continue to explore the link between science and ethics, using examples drawn from community discussions or local newspapers.

Meteorology continues to be a subject of study, as does energy. Children become fairly sophisticated about weather patterns, wind directions, temperature, precipitation, air pressure with high and low systems, hydroelectric power, the link between fuel and electricity, and so on. They will be able to examine weather maps, follow weather reports on television, and understand utility bills.

The intermediate years are a good time for classes to regularly visit science museums, or for scientists and technologists to visit classrooms. Children need to be exposed to these experiences, which will widen their science horizons, give them new questions to ponder, and show them how real people set about solving science problems. These exposures to concrete experience relate directly to one of the major

goals of science study in the sixth grade: the use of scientific understanding to predict and explain various phenomena.

Inquiry—an open-ended approach to the study of science—has a
large role in the sixth grade. Children will be asked to engage in the
process of inquiry, experimenting with ways of finding answers both
to their own questions and to questions posed by the teacher. Such
questions might include: Why do we see better in daytime than at
night? What shapes or designs will support the most weight? Why do
some objects stand and others fall? How can I get my glider to fly
farther? Or not spin so much? Or land more smoothly? How much
of the school's waste is recyclable? How old are the trees in the school
yard? How about the trees along the river? What are the differences
between a pig's liver and a human liver? Why does hot air rise? How
could a species of fish be introduced into a new ecosystem, as when
coho salmon were introduced into the Great Lakes? Children's
questions are unending, and good teachers use those questions to
teach students about the process of inquiry—how to go about examining something. The children thus do what scientists do: define a
problem and then figure out how to solve it.

In regard to the study of health, children continue the exploration of
the life cycle that was begun in the earlier grades. What it means to
stay healthy—to maintain wellness—cannot be overemphasized.
Sixth grade children will continue to pay attention to life-style choices
such as smoking, and they learn about the effects of various kinds of
consumption upon health as well as upon the environment. They also
learn something about medicine and its effect on health. And because
many, if not most, sixth graders have reached puberty, attention is
given to bodily changes.

In many schools sixth grade children receive fairly concrete information about human reproduction, AIDS, and condoms within a framework of personal responsibility. Programs of this nature are sometimes controversial, and some parents and educators question whether topics such as birth control and sexually transmitted diseases should be introduced. But most of the programs of this nature that I have observed are extremely sensitive to the children's developmental status and cultural backgrounds. In the best settings, the teachers who present the material have received training in how to assess students' readiness to receive the information and how to communicate it effectively. Schools that offer such programs usually try to maintain close communication with individual parents and parents' groups; if your child is going to learn about sexuality and reproduction in school, you will be aware of it—and you will have a voice in determining what material is to be presented, and how. You and your child can approach these sensitive topics by reading books together. For example, you can prepare your child to talk about AIDS by reading one of these books: *When Heroes Die* by Penny Durant, *AIDS: How It Works in the Body* by Lorne Greenberg, or *My Own Story* by Ryan White with Mary Moore Cunningham.

SOCIAL STUDIES

History and geography are distinct fields of study in the sixth grade, as they were in the fifth grade, although they should be linked whenever possible to what is being studied in language arts and in science. Sixth grade children are able to use several different kinds of maps; to use primary sources—historical records, diaries, newspapers, and the like—to enlarge their understanding of other people and other time periods; and to interview their parents and grandparents about other times. These skills are enhanced during the intermediate grades as children continue to work with maps and primary documents, and as they become involved in active inquiry to answer questions they have posed.

At the same time, children gain more sophistication about the framing of historical questions: Why did that happen? What are the facts? Are the sources reliable? What are the interpretations? What other possibilities were there? What were the effects? How do we know? How have things changed or stayed the same since then? Whose voice is not being heard?

The sixth grade curriculum typically concentrates on ancient history and world geography; it includes information about the origins and growth of Judaism, Christianity, and Islam. But in the best classrooms, the social studies curriculum also continues to follow current events in the nation and the world. Furthermore, the teacher uses the children's interests as the springboard for investigations into their origins in Europe, Africa, Asia, or Latin America. Whenever possible, social studies also highlights legends, those mythical stories that have been handed down across the generations. The mythologies of Egypt, Greece, and Rome, for example, add great vitality to social studies at this level. Children in the intermediate and middle school years tend to be attracted to the mythic, and mythic stories can teach much about various peoples and cultures.

Regarding ancient history, children will learn how archaeologists and historians have pieced together accounts of life in various early civilizations; how civil governments were formed; how various peoples interacted and cultures grew; the role of religion in ancient societies, and the like. Special attention is paid to the roots of democracy in the city-states of Greece and in Rome.

As part of their study of history, children will visit historical sites and museums. But teachers will foster the recognition that history is more than just a collection of facts and dates—that it is the story of everyday life and ordinary people as well as of blockbuster events and famous individuals. Finally, teachers will encourage the children to read the daily newspaper, watch news on television, and talk regularly with their parents or guardians about local, state, national, and world events.

THE ARTS

Experience with the arts is important throughout elementary school. Children often have specialist art teachers, especially in the intermediate grades. These twice-weekly sessions are most often devoted to vocal music, which is certainly beneficial; yet it would be far better if the arts program also included regular sessions of dance, painting, and instrumental music. The arts have an unstable history in our schools—arts programs are sometimes viewed as less important than other programs, and they are often among the first to be cut when budgets are tight. Parents should therefore be vigilant, insisting that strong, balanced arts programs are essential and must be made available to their children.

Ideally, the classroom time devoted to the arts program is supplemented by after-school enrichment programs and small group lessons, particularly in music and the visual arts. The intermediate years are an especially fertile time for children who are interested in string instruments. Throughout the intermediate grades, children are readily drawn to painting as a means of self-expression, and they are also attracted to group choral singing.

Visits to art museums and attendance at musical performances are a regular part of the curriculum. And discussions on the arts are incorporated into all areas of study. For example, in social studies, much can be learned about ancient Egypt from an examination of the crafts, sculpture, and jewelry of the age of the pharaohs. And instructive comparisons can be made among the architectural structures of Egypt, Greece, and Rome. Teachers can also integrate the arts into the curriculum by having the children read biographies of musicians, dancers, and painters as part of their language arts work; children can also read the lyrics of both classical and contemporary songs. Another way children gain enhanced awareness of the arts is by putting on plays or concerts for which they design and paint sets and write scripts and music. In social studies, the arts are introduced as cultural aspects of life—for example, various art forms can be related to their regions of origin. Even science touches the arts when topics such as sound and color appear in the science curriculum.

Teachers and parents should encourage sixth grade children to watch performance programs on public television; these broadcasts can do a great deal to enrich children's knowledge and appreciation of a wide range of music and drama. So can visits to rehearsals of high school orchestras and dance and theater groups. Even opera can be quite accessible and enjoyable to a child, if care is taken to tell the child what to expect and how to interpret what he or she views.

5

Conversations with Your Child

This chapter presents an array of "conversation starters" for you to use with your sixth grade child. I use the term *conversation* broadly, to include both question-and-answer dialogues and a variety of games and activities. The conversation starters are grouped by subject matter: the language arts and the creative arts, math, science and health, and social studies. Most of the ideas and suggestions I offer are broad and open-ended; some, however, are quite specific. And many of the conversation starters can be adapted and expanded by imaginative parents (and children) for an almost infinite number of possibilities.

Some of the conversations that are introduced in this volume of the *101 Educational Conversations* series appeared in the earlier volume, *101 Educational Conversations You Should Have with Your Fifth Grader*. Most of these, however, have been reframed to accommodate the greater maturity and knowledge of the sixth grader. Such overlapping will also occur in later volumes of the series. In part this overlapping occurs because the curriculum is often interconnected from year to year. But the overlap also reflects the developmental character of learning—the same ideas are right for different children at different ages. And returning to the same conversations or activities a year or more from now will let you see how your child's knowledge and understanding have grown.

During the intermediate grades, factual information begins to take on ever greater importance in your child's education. Each year's curriculum reflects the growing importance of a knowledge base, and so, therefore, do the conversations I offer as your child progresses through school. Nonetheless, the factual information should not be viewed as an end in itself. The learning process itself—and the mental and emotional qualities that promote effective learning—continue to be of paramount importance, but your educational conversations with your child will inevitably involve more and more information and deeper levels of understanding. Do not let this prospect alarm you—it is *not* necessary that you always know more than your child or that you know the answer to every question your child asks. Indeed, you should expect your child to know more than you about a variety of subjects that he or she is studying in school. You can learn a lot from your children and a lot about their education simply by asking them to share their growing knowledge base with you. By encouraging your child with comments such as "I don't understand that—could you explain it to me?" you can do much to strengthen his or her understanding of the subject in question, and perhaps your own understanding as well.

Do not be discouraged if some of the conversations and activities in this and later books appear to require knowledge that you do not have at your fingertips. It is not always necessary for you to know the answer to a question that you pose to your child; in fact, sometimes it is both more fun and more helpful to the child for the two of you to look up the answer together. You may, though, want to familiarize yourself with some basic reference tools, either at home or at your library: a dictionary, an encyclopedia, and an atlas would be good places to start. You can also read through your child's schoolbooks. The schools could contribute to this process as well by presenting occasional parents' workshops, at which parents can get "refresher courses" in the subject matter their children are studying. The conversation starters that follow are a way for you to discover what your child knows and understands in relation to what is typically taught in the schools. You should remember, however, that the curriculum is not identical in every school; a gap in your child's learning may simply mean that that particular subject has not yet been introduced in the classroom. Be satisfied if your child can engage in *most* of these conversations, even with partial knowledge or limited understanding. You can always return to problem areas later on, as your child's mastery increases. But what about areas of learning that appear to be entirely outside a child's knowledge? A sixth grade child, for example, may appear to know very little about poetry, either how to read it or how to write it. While poetry is part of the curriculum in most schools, I do not believe that this particular gap in knowledge is necessarily a serious problem; parents themselves can help children with this kind of learning by reading and writing poetry together. But the parents might, nonetheless, ask the child's teacher, "What are you doing to help the children read and write poetry?" On the other hand, if a sixth grade child shows little interest in any kind of writing or is struggling to make sense of a graph, the parents should certainly talk with the teacher, even as they spend more time writing with their child and looking at graphs together.

The following ideas have been framed as conversational exchanges or playful interactions, not as daily quizzes. They are designed to promote interaction between parents and children. And because conversation does not flourish when questions lend themselves to simple answers—"yes," "no," and "I don't know"—most of the questions and activities have an open-ended quality. Try not to make them seem like tests or like some form of Trivial Pursuit. Instead, work them naturally into the time you spend with your child. The conversations should occur in a relaxed, comfortable context—at dinner, during a walk or a game, perhaps in relation to shared television programs or movies, or at some quiet time.

Many parents of sixth grade children discover that children passing through the intermediate years are less and less available for the kinds of conversations that occurred between parents and younger children. In part this is because older children tend to be involved in a greater variety of activities with peers and outside the home than younger children. But it also reflects the child's natural development: as children approach their teens and begin to establish separate identities, they are simply less and less interested in talking and playing games with their parents. Except in extreme cases this is not cause for alarm or dismay. But you should be aware that you may find it difficult to engage in regular, sustained educational conversations with your sixth grade child.

Do not give up, however. Be as flexible and natural as possible, and use external factors—movies, television, the newspaper, and especially your child's own observations about school, homework, and the like—as springboards into the conversations. And use the conversations that follow as a window into your child's intellectual development: They will give you a good idea of the kinds of knowledge and skills your child should be mastering. If the child's overall level of intellectual activity seems to lag significantly behind that of these conversations, you should look more closely at his or her curriculum and discuss the matter with the teacher.

In a fundamental way, these conversations are educational opportunities. They allow you not only to reinforce what your child's teacher is doing but to expand the teacher's efforts, enriching your child's education. I believe that parents will, in the process of engaging in the conversations, realize more fully that they too are important and capable teachers. An additional benefit is that parents who take part in these exchanges will show their children that learning is a valuable activity, one that is capable of providing pleasure and is worthy of respect.

The conversations are built around some important assumptions. I have assumed that parents:

- Read to their children frequently.

- Listen to their children, respond to their questions, and engage them in ongoing conversations.

- Find opportunities to play with their children—physically active games as well as board and card games.

- Take walks with their children—around the block, through the parks, to a local playground.

- Take their children to the library, zoos, museums, and nature trails.

- Listen to records and tapes with their children.

- Let their children help them cook, wash the car, or tend a garden.

- Watch television with their children and discuss the content of programs with them.

- Share family stories with their children.

By enjoying their children regularly and naturally in the course of these and other activities, parents come to know a great deal about their children's growth as learners. The questions, activities, and ideas in this chapter will tell parents even more about their children—particularly about what their children are learning in school.

As you go through these conversations, keep in mind that sixth grade children are being exposed to a great deal of information in school and are still in the process of consolidating many ideas and relationships. Moreover, they are trying to make sense of what they are learning, striving for deeper understanding and for mastery of skills. If, for example, children learn various science facts but cannot use them for purposes they actually understand, can- not make connections between the facts and the world they see around them, then science is not becoming a particularly important subject matter. For science and for all subject areas, true understanding is far more important than a jumble of factual information that has little use beyond school and does not lead to more accelerated learning.

All-Purpose Conversation Starters

Many conversations between you and your child can arise spontaneously from day-to-day events. You can create numerous opportunities for such interactions in the following ways:

- Look at all the materials your child brings home from school. You will see a variety of things, including work sheets, word lists, books, classification exercises, writing samples, projects in progress, sculptures, paintings, and sketches. Ask your child about them. Say, "This looks interesting. Can you tell me how you did it?" or "I see you are learning about Greek mythology. What are you finding particularly interesting? What have you learned about Zeus and Apollo?" Remember to be supportive rather than judgmental. If your child does not regularly bring writing, books, drawings, constructions, experiments, or paintings home from school, you should be concerned.

- Take note of your child's games and conversations with other family members and with friends. By looking closely at what your child brings home from school, the books your child selects from the library, and how your child acts out new knowledge or skills while playing, you can keep in touch with elements of your child's education. These observations form a significant part of what you know about your child.

Certain questions that promote conversation between you and your child are versatile enough to apply in just about any situation. They may already be part of your repertoire. If not, start working them into your conversations. Use them often, but always—to repeat a point I made earlier in this chapter—use them patiently and naturally.

The questions are: "I wonder why that is?" "What do you think is happening?" "Is there any other way to do it?" "What if you tried it that way?" These questions and the many variations you can invent not only help keep dialogue going but also stimulate inquiry and discovery.

Language and the Arts

Throughout the intermediate and middle school years, children need to maintain confidence in their ability to read and write. The biggest keys to effective reading and writing are practice and exposure to a broad range of language and its uses; this is how children expand their understanding of what language can do. The schools will contribute to this learning through the stories teachers read, the records and tapes children listen to, and the many intentional elaborations of words and word meanings teachers provide. But the home is also important. Read a broad range of literature together: rhymes, poems, fables, folktales, classic stories, and biographies. Sing songs together and play games. Such experiences will make a critical difference in your child's learning. In addition, call attention to things in newspapers and magazines, leave written messages around for your child, and make sure that your *own* literacy is evident. It is important for your child to see you reading and writing—and enjoying it.

You should try to do some reading with your child on a regular basis. By now, you know that as your child moves forward through the grades, his or her schedule becomes more active and self-initiated. You have probably found also that it is not as easy as it once was to engage in daily reading together. At a minimum, though, try to spend some time on Sunday afternoons or evenings reading from authors such as Charles Dickens, Robert Louis Stevenson, James Fenimore Cooper, Charlotte Brontë, Jack London, Langston Hughes, Amy Tan, Virginia Sneve, Bret Harte, Alex Haley, Louisa May Alcott, Edith Hamilton, C. S. Lewis, Sally Benson, Harper Lee, or Paul Laurence Dunbar. Your child's interest in the stories you read will tell you a great deal about his or her development in listening and comprehension.

Begin or continue a journal of good times together—possibly the highlights of a trip, vacation, or family holiday; or a log of books and movies you've shared. You and your child can each make entries. From time to time read through what you have written.

Read newspaper headlines together, and try to figure out what the story is about. You might also make a point of reading aloud to each other one newspaper story every day. This will help make the newspaper important to your child as well as provide reading practice. In addition, you will learn a great deal about your child's growing knowledge of the world. This is a good activity to share on a regular basis as it does not take a great deal of time.

Get in the habit of clipping from the newspaper things you think your child might find interesting—human interest stories, cartoons, movie or television reviews, news related to the local environment. Also call your child's attention to articles in magazines. Such pieces are natural starting points for conversation.

Committing things to memory is a good exercise throughout the intermediate and middle school years. At one time, schoolchildren were expected to memorize many poems. Although this is not typical of most schools any longer, memorization still has some virtues. At home each of you could memorize a poem or story to tell to the other—one in the fall and one in the spring. The presentations can be made into traditional family events.

Mystery and adventure tend to attract sixth grade readers. Visit together the sections of your library where mysteries and adventure stories are shelved; each of you could pick something to read and discuss with the other.

Buy books for your child for special occasions. This is a way to tell your child that you value reading and ideas. It also gives you a chance to build later conversations around the books you have bought, by asking, "How was the book? What was the mystery?" and the like. *South & North, East & West: The Oxfam Book of Children's Stories*, edited by Michael Rosen, offers 25 traditional tales from all parts of the world that can provide a great deal of shared pleasure for you and your child.

As your child reads, find time to ask, "What is the book about? Who are the characters? What are they like? Where does the story take place?" Most children like to talk about what they are reading, as long as they do not perceive the questions to be either suspicious inquisitions or rote inquiries devoid of real interest.

Take your child to the movies occasionally—rather than just sending him or her to the movies. You will not only enjoy the outing together, but the event will give you a natural opportunity for conversation about the film's characters, setting, theme, moral dilemmas, and so on. Such conversations not only enlarge your child's understanding of the film but may go beyond the movie itself to a broad range of subjects.

Each of you write an explanation of how to do something. For example, your child might decide to write a description of how to climb a tree or play a particular musical instrument, while you will describe how to bake an apple pie or replace a windowpane. Then see if your descriptions make sense to one another. Would your child's explanation help someone climb a tree for the first time?

As you read your child's writing, ask yourself the following questions. The answers will help you evaluate his or her progress.

- Is it focused? Is the central point clear?

- Are the ideas presented in reasonably sequential order from beginning to end?

- Is enough information given to show that your child understands the subject he or she has written about?

- Does the writing reveal some personal interest in the subject?

- Are the ideas expressed in complete sentences?

- Has the child used a variety of sentence structures, both simple and complex, or do all the sentences sound the same?

- Do the child's choices of vocabulary and grammar reflect standard usage?

- Is the writing punctuated correctly?

Write each other persuasive letters, telling why each of you thinks that the other should do something. (This could be good fun.) Compare what you both write to similar letters you might have written last year. Has your child's mastery of persuasive language improved?

See what your child knows about the playwright William Shakespeare. (He or she is likely to be familiar with the plays *Hamlet* and *Julius Caesar*.) Try reading some Shakespeare together.

By the sixth grade your child should be a reasonably confident speller. Ask what words he or she has trouble spelling. See if together you can devise some mnemonic trick to aid in remembering the correct spelling. (The old rule "i before e, except after c" is an example of a mnemonic device; so is "stalagmite has a g because it grows from the ground, stalactite has a c because it hangs from the ceiling.")

Keep doing crossword puzzles together, steadily moving on to more complex puzzles. Children's sections of newspapers often have crosswords for children; many books of children's puzzles are also available. You may find, however, that by sixth grade your child is ready to do the regular newspaper puzzle.

Listen to many different kinds of music together. Share your views about the music; find something in the lyrics to talk about. This will help your child enjoy music and also let you watch your child's music awareness grow. It is not unusual for children in the intermediate and middle grades to become strongly interested in new contemporary music, with which you may not be familiar. Your child will probably enjoy sharing his or her favorite popular music with you if your attitude is neither judgmental nor condescending. The important thing is to stay in touch with your child's *interest* in music, not to criticize his or her particular choices.

Orchestras contain sections for different types of instruments. Ask your child what instruments he or she would find in the wind section (flute, piccolo, clarinet, saxophone), the brass section (trumpet, trombone, French horn), and the string section (violin, viola, cello).

See what your child is learning about *perspective* in painting. If your child's class has studied ancient art, particularly Egyptian art, he or she will probably know something about how ancient artists showed distance and size.

As a language-expanding conversation that will also tell you how much your child knows about many aspects of the world, say, "Let's tell each other all we know about Alexander the Great." (Or George Washington Carver, Mark Twain, hurricanes, Nubian culture, apartheid, the Yankton Sioux Indians, Mycenaean civilization, Mars, particular cities, the space shuttles, Odysseus, Cicero, atomic energy, airplanes, different parts of the world, and so on.) You can see what words, people, and concepts are familiar to your child and also introduce new ones. This kind of activity is almost limitless. But you must listen carefully to your child's expressions. Do not be too hasty to correct or interrupt with information you think your child should know; that can come later, at the end of the activity or in a different conversation. It is important to let children express themselves fully instead of immediately quenching their pleasure with corrections.

Each of you take turns thinking of words that describe something. For example, if you chose "a warm, humid day" as your subject, the adjectives you come up with might include *sweltering, wet, sticky, stifling, lazy*, and so on. This type of wordplay has almost limitless possibilities. It is a good chance for your child to experiment with his or her new vocabulary words and for you to see how your child's descriptive skills are growing.

Can your child distinguish between a simile (a comparison using *like* or *as*, such as "a heart as big as all outdoors") and a metaphor (a comparison that equates one thing with another, such as "all the world's a stage")?

We use a variety of conventions to talk about literature. Ask your child to explain to you what setting, plot, theme, and point of view are.

Take turns describing an object, a person, an event, a situation. Such an activity provides good practice in observation and in the precise use of descriptive language. Look for stories or essays in which things are vividly described and share these passages with each other.

Authorship is an important part of reading and writing. Talk with your child about new books and their authors. Check out new titles through book reviews in the children's section of the newspaper or in the library. Many local libraries sponsor events where authors speak about their work or give readings from it; attend some of these with your child.

Your child will be doing many different kinds of writing in school. The emphasis will be on narrative writing (about something that happened), descriptive writing (using details to help the reader visualize a scene), and explanatory writing (explaining something). Ask your child to tell you about these different kinds of writing and when he or she might use each one.

Keep encouraging your child to write stories and poems for friends and family members. Children in the intermediate and middle school years should also be encouraged to keep a journal, diary, or memory book; these activities not only give children writing practice but allow them to discover writing as a means of self-expression.

Invite your child to read one of his or her stories, poems, essays, or journal entries to you while it is in progress (this will reinforce experiences your child is having with writing in school). When your child shares his or her ongoing work, you can gently let the child see whether the writing conveys what he or she wants it to. In addition, hearing your child's work at various stages both reinforces the point that revision is a natural part of writing and lets you watch your child's progress over time.

Look at paintings together, either at museums or in books and magazines; this is an inexpensive activity and one you should share as often as possible. Van Gogh, Gauguin, Picasso, and Matisse have a great deal of appeal. You might also give some attention to abstract and geometric art. Ask your child what he or she likes about various paintings. Also ask about art activities in school. What is your child learning about painters, sculptors, and museum collections?

Ask often how your child likes various artworks—paintings, architecture, photographs, and music. This is your way of saying that you value artistic expression and of keeping your child's interest high.

Read plays aloud together, taking various parts. Turn holidays or family parties into occasions for dramatic readings or plays acted out at home. Your local library should have a children's theater or drama section. See how your child approaches reading a script.

Make sure you watch together at least one arts-related television program each week. Check your public television station for such programs as "The American Experience," "Great Performances," "The Boston Pops," and the like. Ask your child what he or she particularly liked (or disliked) about the program? If your child has questions about the work that was performed, the two of you can research the answers together.

Inquire about phrases your child is learning in other languages. Does he or she know any phrases in Latin, French, Spanish, Japanese?

Read favorite poems aloud to each other. Poetry is the oldest form of literature, and it is still powerful and popular. It can also greatly expand a child's understanding of language.

Suggest that your child write a letter to a public official or an organization about a cause that concerns him or her—to the mayor of your city about safety in local parks or the need for bike paths, for example. Both the conventions of this type of letter and the importance of speaking out on issues should be a part of your child's curriculum.

Throughout their schooling children should be encouraged to assess their own progress as learners. In relation to reading and the language arts, ask your child such questions as, "How is your writing coming along?" "What causes you difficulty?" "What do you most enjoy about writing?" "Are you finding new authors whose work you like a lot?" Your child's responses will give you hints about games, activities, or pastimes to share with your child to boost his or her learning; they will also serve as a starting point for your own conversations with your child's teacher.

Mathematics

Like language, math is a subject in which it is important for children to build and maintain confidence. Sixth grade children continue to study quantities, size, scale, and estimation as they move into geometry and pre-algebra. There is also continuing attention to mastering addition, subtraction, division, and multiplication. Rather than an exclusive focus on whole numbers, however, children work more with fractions, ratios, and percentages. They also do more problem solving with math.

The more concrete the learning, and the more children are encouraged to see mathematics in use all around them, the better. You can help by using math and the language of math around the house. Have your child help you with measuring tasks such as placing a picture on the wall, cutting out a pattern, building shelves, papering a wall, or landscaping. Get your child to make estimates and judgments about distance and time, and play a lot of number-oriented games. Math is a natural area of learning that should always be interesting to children.

Play tic-tac-toe, dots, checkers, dominoes, concentration, hangman, Scrabble, chess, and increasingly complex card games such as hearts, rummy, and cribbage with your child. All involve problem solving and logic, and all are based on mathematics.

Skill in solving problems is one of the goals of mathematical study. Ask your child to show you how he or she goes about solving a word problem in math. (Steps in the process might include trying to understand the question, finding the pertinent information, deciding what to do, working out the answer, and checking the answer.)

Ask your child to determine the best way to solve the following problems, using a calculator, paper and pencil, mental calculation, or estimation:

- We have 12 shelves and we have to put 40 cans on each shelf. How many cans will we need?

- John works at a fast food restaurant and makes $6 an hour. If he works 28 hours each week, how much will he earn in eight weeks?

- A jogger runs 10 kilometers each weekday and 15 kilometers each weekend day. How many kilometers did the jogger run during the past month? (Use your calendar to figure out the number of weekdays and weekend days.)

- A sweatshirt store can print four designs—A, B, X, and Y—on sweatshirts. Each pattern can be printed alone or in combination with any or all of the other designs. If you wanted to own one of every possible design combination, how many sweatshirts would you have to buy? [4+4x4=4x4x4+4x4x4x4]

With a map of the United States, ask, "What is the shortest route from Princeton, New Jersey, to San Francisco, California?" Or from Boston, Massachusetts, to Madison, Wisconsin. Or have your child figure out how long it would take to get to the homes of relatives and friends around the country—or the world—by plane, train, automobile, or on foot. When you travel, make sure to involve your child in planning travel routes.

Ask, "How could we figure out how tall our house is?" What about a local church, or the school? Expect your child to come up with many suggestions for figuring out the height.

Make up problems. For example: "It takes us 5 hours and 15 minutes to get to Aunt Siobhan's house if we average 55 miles an hour. How long would it take if we went 60 miles an hour? How about 50, or 45?"

The calculator should be very familiar to your child. Using a calculator, pick a number such as 109, then take turns adding a number from 1 to 8 into the memory. The objective is to see who can get to 109 first. This is a good mental math task and also another way to use the calculator.

Multiplying three-digit numbers is common in the sixth grade. Children are taught to think of the problem 422 x 396 in this way: 6 x 422, 90 x 422, and 300 x 422. Another way to visualize it is:

```
  422
  396
   2,532 (6 x 422)
  37,980 (90 x 422)
 126,600 (300 x 422)
 167,112
```

Have your child work out the following problems (do them yourself at the same time and compare your solutions with your child's): 508 x 183; 759 x 341; 192 x 546.

Your child has probably learned about a lattice form of multiplication that was used in Italy by the 15th century, and possibly earlier. Using this method, your child would solve the problem 296 x 23 by creating the following lattice:

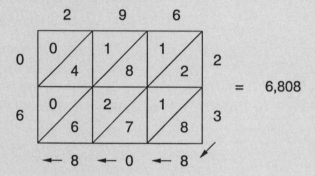

= 6,808

Ask your child to show you how to make lattices for these problems: 592 x 76; 659 x 238; 224 x 32. Discuss whether this method of multiplying is easier or harder than the method described in the previous conversation.

See if your child can think of occasions when dividing numbers would be necessary or helpful. Make up some problems together. For example, "Which is a better buy: four frozen pizzas for $10.88, or 5 for $14.10?" Or, "How many cars would we need to take 36 children to the zoo, if four people could ride in each car?" (Don't forget the driver of each car.)

See how your child approaches problems in division with one- and two-digit divisors. How does he or she handle these problems:

$6\overline{)5056}$, $4\overline{)259}$, $3\overline{)2962}$, $70\overline{)210}$, $70\overline{)6900}$

Ask your child to teach you how to do the problems. Does his or her explanation show an understanding of the basic principles involved?

Sixth graders are learning various metric units of measurement. What does your child know about meters and centimeters (m and cm)? About liters and milliliters (l and ml)? Grams and kilograms (g and kg)? Have your child use meters and centimeters to measure how far he or she can jump, spread his or her fingers, or throw a ball.

Ask your child to explain *volume* to you (this usually involves cubic units of measurement). If a box is 6 centimeters long, 4 cm wide, and 3 cm high, what is its volume? (The answer is: 6 x 4 x 3 = 72 cubic centimeters, or 72 cm^3.) What would be the volume of a train car 6 meters high, 24 m long, and 5 m wide? One liter is equal to 1,000 cubic milliliters, or ml^3; how many milliliters of water would a 3-liter fish tank hold? One kilogram equals 1,000 grams; how many grams are there in 200 kg?

Encourage your child to become familar with the act of striking an average. Weigh a series of objects and record the weight of each. Suppose they weighed 25, 40, 16, 22, 21, 62, and 92 pounds—does your child know how to calculate their average weight? Do the same thing with the length in inches of various objects, the temperatures at a certain time of day over a week, or any other series of numbers.

Ask your child to graph food prices—eggs, chicken, potatoes, and so on—during one week for three consecutive months. (If you did this when your child was in the fifth grade, you can compare last year's prices with this year's.) Your child can check prices either at the store or in advertisements. Do prices go up, go down, or stay the same? See what your child can tell you about how they change. What ideas does he or she have about why such changes occur?

Sixth graders begin to work more intensively with geometry; part of geometry involves the spatial relationships of lines and points. Ask your child to tell you about the lines in the following drawings:

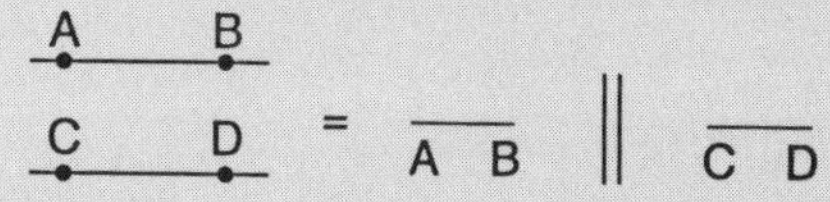

line segment AB
intersects with
line segment CD

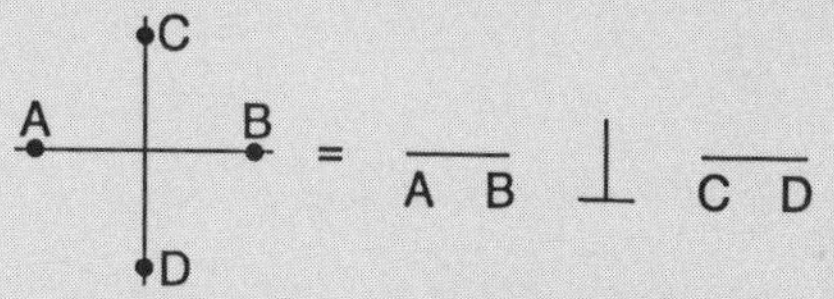

line segment AB
is parallel with
line segment CD

Geometry also involves shapes and angles. Can your child identify the following angles:

= [Right angle (90°)]

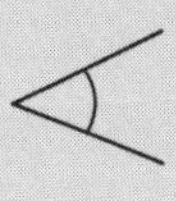

= [Acute angle (less than 90°)]

= [Obtuse angle (more than 90°)]

See if your child can use a protractor to measure the angles in the following triangles:

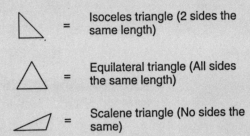

= Isoceles triangle (2 sides the same length)

= Equilateral triangle (All sides the same length)

= Scalene triangle (No sides the same)

Ask your child to draw a square, a rectangle, a parallelogram, a trapezoid, and a rhombus. All are quadrilateral shapes (they have four sides); can your child explain how they differ from one another?

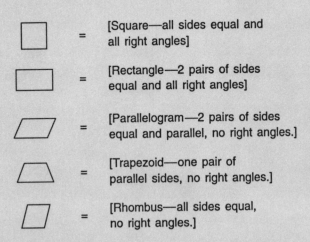

= [Square—all sides equal and all right angles]

= [Rectangle—2 pairs of sides equal and all right angles]

= [Parallelogram—2 pairs of sides equal and parallel, no right angles.]

= [Trapezoid—one pair of parallel sides, no right angles.]

= [Rhombus—all sides equal, no right angles.]

Have your child draw a circle and explain to you its radius, its diameter, and its circumference.

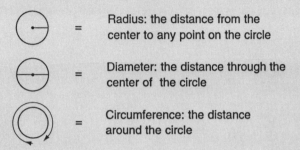

= Radius: the distance from the center to any point on the circle

= Diameter: the distance through the center of the circle

= Circumference: the distance around the circle

Using a compass, each of you draw designs using circles and arcs. Color these according to a repetitive pattern, such as green, red, blue, green, red, and so on.

See whether your child can draw shapes in three dimensions—cubes, spheres, and the like.

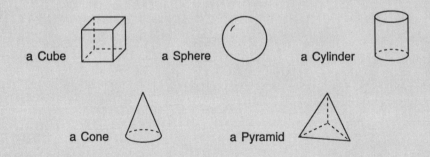

a Cube   a Sphere   a Cylinder

a Cone   a Pyramid

You and your child should be able to find geometric shapes throughout the house and the environment outside the house. For example, windows and windowpanes are usually rectangles, oranges and globes are spheres, flour and sugar canisters may be cylinders, and angles exist wherever walls and ceilings come together. Make a game of seeing how many geometric shapes you can identify in a five-minute period, or in the course of a walk together.

Your child should be gaining confidence in the use of ratios. See what he or she can do with these problems:

- Three of every four people in our community voted for John Jones for Congress. Of the 1,680 people who voted, how many voted for Jones?

- Two of every nine students at a nearby college are African-American. How many of the 800 students are African-American?

By sixth grade the interchange from fractions to percentages, or from percentages to fractions, should be commonplace for your child. Can he or she translate these fractions into percentages: 1/10, 1/3, 2/7, 1/4, 1/5, 5/8? How about changing these percentages into fractions: .25, .75, .50, .17, .35, .90?

Combine geometry and multiplication or division in problems for your child to solve. For example, "If the diameter of the earth is 8,000 miles, how fast would you have to travel to make it around the earth in 80 days?" (In this case your child will first have to work out the circumference of the earth, using the diameter as the starting point, and then divide that distance by 80.)

Ask your child to list the first five numbers that end in 5 (5, 15, 25, 35, 45) and then to square each number. This should result in the following series: 25, 225, 625, 1225, 2025. What does your child notice about these numbers? All of them end in 25, and what precedes the 25 increases in a pattern of 2, 4, 6, 8. Would that pattern continue for the sixth number ending in 5? The seventh? The eighth? Have your child square 55, 65, and 75 and see what happens.

Your sixth grade child should be fairly sophisticated in the use of graphs—both making them and reading them. Ask him or her to make a circle or pie graph of time spent during the previous week, with sections representing school, watching TV, sleeping, playing with friends, reading, doing homework, and the like.

See if your child can produce a bar graph that shows how far away relatives or friends live. (This exercise will probably require some map studying and some computing of distance as well as preparation of the graph itself.) Other subjects for bar graphs could include the heights or ages of family members.

Ask your child, "How well do you understand the math you are studying in school? What are you having difficulty with? Do you think you need help? What kind of help would be best?" Again, your child's responses may guide your interactions with both the child and his or her teacher.

Occasionally ask your child, "Is there anything you wish you knew about math that you aren't learning?"

Using the values assigned to letters in Scrabble (listed below), try to come up with words that have high values. Turn this into a game, where each of you tries to top the other's word.

A = 1	J = 8	S = 1
B = 3	K = 5	T = 1
C = 3	L = 1	U = 1
D = 2	M = 3	V = 4
E = 1	N = 1	W = 4
F = 4	O = 1	X = 8
G = 2	P = 3	Y = 4
H = 4	Q = 10	Z = 10
I = 1	R = 1	

SCIENCE AND HEALTH

Science study in the sixth grade remains concerned with the natural world—wind and rain, ponds, rivers, lakes, streams, the solar system, animals and plants, and food chains—though technology takes on added importance. At this point the students become increasingly aware of the physical and life sciences and specialized fields of inquiry. They should know, for example, how *zoology* differs from *botany*, and how both differ from *geology*.

Sixth grade students observe nature and learn how things move through their various life cycles; they also observe various aspects of technology and learn about its development, uses, and problems. The intermediate grades are an important time for keeping curiosity alive and helping children expand their observation and problem-solving skills.

Observe the moon together over several weeks; note whether you are looking at it at the same time every day or at different times. (You and your child could do this exercise once a year for several years—perhaps at a different season each year—and learn something new each time.) Note the moon's location and draw its various shapes; be aware of the stars around it. Examine the moon chart in the weather section of your daily newspaper or on a calendar. There is almost no end to the astronomical observations you and your child can make. If, like many parents, you are not especially familiar with the sky, this exercise will be a good learning experience for you as well as for your child.

Ask about the scientists your child is currently studying. Are men and women represented? What about people of color? What does your child know about these scientists and their work?

What does your child know about the effects of caffeine, tobacco, alcohol, marijuana, cocaine, heroin? Keep in touch with what your child is learning about drugs and drug abuse. Does he or she show a growing awareness of drugs as a problem? You should be aware that many sixth graders are beginning to experiment with drugs. Your local library or a counselor can suggest books that will help prepare you to discuss this subject with your child.

See what your child knows about the digestive system. Ask, "How does food change as we digest it?"

What does your child know about the different functions of red and white blood cells? (The red carry oxygen; the white fight infection.)

Ask what happens when we inhale and exhale. (Inhaling draws oxygen into the body; exhaling expels carbon dioxide.)

Science study in the sixth grade continues to give attention to the sources of common things and to everyday processes. You and your child can investigate questions such as "Why do magnets pick up some metals and not others?" "How does electricity travel?" "How are movies made?"

Your child is studying the role of technology in society. Ask about how television has changed people's lives. What was daily life like before television (not all that long ago)? You can also talk about how medical research is keeping people alive longer, and how robots are doing much of the work in automobile factories.

Go birdwatching (or bird counting) with a local nature group. Invest in a paperback pocket guide to the bird species commonly seen in your area; together you and your child can learn how to identify species and study their habits. Each time you go to a park, a wildlife preserve, or a bird sanctuary you will learn something new about birds. Your child—and you—may discover a lifetime of enjoyment in observing nature.

Inquire about the local ecosystem. What does your child know about the food chain and how local species of birds, fish, insects, and mammals fit into it?

Ask your child about the science experiments he or she is doing in school. Have your child describe them: not just what was done but what was learned.

Ask your child to explain the following terms used in science: *observation* (gathering information through the senses), *inference* (a conclusion based on information that may not yet be complete), *assumption* (a belief that something is true, although it is not yet proven), and *interpretation* (giving meaning to observations and information).

Your child is learning a good deal about plant life in school. Ask why leaves turn yellow and red in the fall (they lose chlorophyll, the substance that gives them their green color).

Movies, television shows, and books will offer plenty of chances to structure conversations around the subject of space flight. What does your child know about rockets, acceleration, weightlessness, orbits, comets, asteroids, and stellar constellations?

The planets were named after Greek and Roman gods and goddesses. Can your child identify the sources of these names: Mercury (messenger of the gods), Venus (goddess of love), Mars (god of war), Jupiter (father and leader of the gods), Saturn (god of agriculture), Neptune (god of the sea), Uranus (god of the heavens), and Pluto (god of the underworld)?

See what your child knows about hunger in the world today. A discussion about why hunger exists could take many directions: nutrition and the number of calories needed to sustain life, environmental damage and loss of farmland, or politics and aid programs.

Watch nature programs on television with your child. These programs offer opportunities for interesting conversations about everything from volcanic eruptions in Mexico to the birds and plants of the Florida Everglades. Your child's level of interest—and the questions he or she asks—are good indications of what the child is learning in school about nature and geography.

Talk with your child about the importance of paying attention to the fat, protein, carbohydrates, cholesterol, and caffeine in our foods. Make a practice of reading nutrition labels together when you are shopping for or preparing food. Ask your child what he or she is learning about nutrition in school.

Ask, "What relationship exists between the moon and the ocean tides?"

See what your child knows about the following scientific concepts: *proton* (a positive electrical charge), *cell* (the smallest form of living matter), *light year* (the distance light travels in a year), *arteries* (blood vessels that carry blood away from the heart), and *large intestine* (stores undigested food).

Can your child distinguish between deciduous and coniferous trees? (Deciduous trees, such as oaks and maples, shed their leaves in the fall; conifers, such as spruce and pine, retain their leaves all year.)

Ask, "Why is it colder in the mountains than at sea level?"

Discuss chemical reactions with your child. For example, what happens when iron and oxygen react? (Rust, or iron oxide, forms.) What does H_2O mean? (Two parts of hydrogen and one part of oxygen form water.) How about CO_2? (Carbon dioxide—one part carbon to two parts oxygen.)

Visit a planetarium with your child. Try to go several times a year, as the programs generally change with the seasons. Before you go, discuss the program to see what your child already knows. After the show, talk about what each of you learned. Let your child see that you, as an adult, keep learning new things; this instills an appreciation of learning as a lifelong process.

The environment continues to be part of the curriculum in the sixth grade. Keep asking your child about things we can do to ensure a healthy environment. Call his or her attention to articles about environmental issues in newspapers and magazines; these are good starting points for conversations, which will show you how your child's understanding of these issues is expanding.

Geology is full of very large numbers. Your child will be reading and hearing about such things as "1 million years before humans appeared on earth" and "4 billion years ago." Discuss these and other big numbers. For example, ask your child how old he or she was 4 million minutes ago (there are 526,000 minutes in a year). Or ask what year it would be if we went back in time 1 million hours (there are 8,760 hours in a year, so 1 million hours would be approximately 114.25 years).

Ask your child about the source of drinking water in your community. What does he or she know about how water is treated to make it safe to drink? Ask how your child would go about checking the purity of the water in local streams and rivers.

Continue encouraging your child to examine his or her own learning. Ask, "How well do you understand the science you are learning in school? Is there anything you don't understand? What would you like to know more about?"

Social Studies

In the sixth grade, as in the earlier grades, the social studies continue to examine relationships within families and communities. At the same time, sixth graders give increasing attention to world geography and the history of the ancient world. In most schools, the early civilizations of Egypt, the Near East, India, and Central America, as well as the classical civilizations of Greece and Rome, make up the focus of sixth grade social studies. A child's work in social studies, as in the other subject areas, should be as concrete and visible in the world as possible. Many of the stories that are read to children, or that children read for themselves, have social studies' themes.

Watch the television news together regularly. Let the events on the news —human interest stories, hurricanes, elections, and the peoples and circumstances of other countries—become a basis for conversation. You might also watch documentaries about historical figures with your child; biography is a good basis for helping children learn about history. Such documentaries are becoming more common, especially on public television and certain cable networks. Documentary programs are also available on videocassette and can be checked out of libraries and rented from many video stores.

Ask what would happen if the oil-producing countries agreed to sell only one-half as much oil as they now sell. (The price of oil and of many other goods would probably increase dramatically.)

Many cities have nicknames. Can your child identify the following: the Motor City (Detroit), the Windy City (Chicago), the City of Angels (Los Angeles), the City by the Bay (San Francisco)?

Children in the intermediate grades will notice and ask about the problems that they see around them: homelessness, drugs, conflict. It is good to talk about these issues. Ask your child whether he or she is discussing such topics in school. Does your child have unanswered questions?

See what your child has to say about why countries need laws, and about why people and countries fight.

Inquire about the work of demographers (specialists who keep track of population growth, habits and beliefs, trends, and the like). Look at some census data about your community and discuss its meaning. What does it tell you about race? Income? Education?

Have your child place various events in chronological order. Try the following events: the Renaissance, the Middle Ages, the Reformation, the Roman Empire *or* the Babylonian Empire, the travels of Marco Polo, the city-states of Athens and Sparta, the Punic Wars between Carthage and Rome.

See if your child can identify some of the following names related to the ancient civilizations of Egypt, Greece, and Rome: Hippocrates, Homer, Julius Caesar, Aristotle, Alexander the Great, Moses, Osiris, and Isis.

Sixth graders study religious traditions. Ask your child to tell you about the Old Testament source of the Ten Commandments, monotheism and the Hebrews, Muhammad and the Koran, Jesus and the origins of Christianity, and Gautama Buddha and the origins of Buddhism.

As part of your child's study of the ancient world, he or she will learn about the civilization of early Egypt. Ask about the Egyptian practice of preserving the bodies of the dead (mummies). How were mummies prepared? (With surgery, chemical solutions, and cloth wrappings.) Why did the Egyptians do this? (They believed that people would need their bodies in the afterlife.)

Your child is learning about the work of archaeologists. Ask what archaeologists do. Discuss how an archaeologist of the future might describe the people who live in your house, based on the artifacts that exist there.

What does your child know about the early history of writing? (His or her answer might touch on the cuneiform tablets of the Sumerians and the hieroglyphic writing of the Egyptians.)

What can your child tell you about the Phoenicians, the Egyptians, the Greeks? Does he or she seem to have a sense of how these peoples helped shape the modern world?

Ask your child to place the following persons in historical order: King Tutankhamen, Alexander the Great, Muhammad, Jesus, Homer.

Keep talking with your child about other countries, perhaps reading about them in a magazine article or an encyclopedia.

Ask your child to share with you what he or she is learning about different ethnic and cultural groups in the United States. What has your child learned about African Americans, Hispanics, Vietnamese, and Cambodians? Is your child reading books and stories by or about members of these groups?

Can your child distinguish between *fact* and *opinion*? Each of you make a statement; the other will say whether the statement is fact or opinion.

The printing press revolutionized communication and society. What does your child know about Johann Gutenberg? About how books were made before the printing press? About the effects of the printing press?

Can your child order the following countries from the most to the least populated: India, France, Japan, China, Canada?

See how many countries you and your child can name in the following world regions: South America, Africa, the Middle East. Take turns naming countries.

Can your child order the following cities from the largest to the smallest population: Chicago, Los Angeles, New York City, Boston, Miami?

Look at a map of the United States with your child. Take turns finding particular cities and towns. Once you have found a town, ask your child how he or she would get there from home. How long might the trip take? Does either of you know something interesting about the town? Each of you could find information about a place and share your information with the other.

Keep up the habit of asking your child, "What do you think?" about events and activities—politics, famine, protests, and issues such as animal rights. Listen carefully to your child's responses. This tells you a great deal about what your child understands. It also tells your child that his or her opinions mean something.

You and your child each make a time line, starting with the year of your birth and listing significant events in your life and important things that happened to you and in the world around you. This enjoyable shared activity not only gives you a chance to put your own life and your child's in historical perspective but it allows you to share milestones in your life with your child.

Your child is learning about travelers in the ancient world: the Phoenician seafarers, the soldiers of Alexander, and so on. Ask, "Do you know how these long-ago travelers stored food? What they ate? How they dressed?"

Engage in community service activities together. Work at a food shelter, or contribute time to various charities. Many charitable organizations and medical research groups sponsor walks as fund raisers, and you and your child could take part in one of these events. Such activities are a chance to discuss the importance of service as part of citizenship.

Visit historical museums or sites together; such sites can be revisited at different points in the child's education. During these visits, talk about how people lived in other times. What are the differences between past and present ways of life? What are the similarities?

Ask your child to teach you something he or she has learned in school.

The news is full of struggles for freedom in various parts of the world. Inquire about your child's understanding of these events. Can he or she compare them with similar events in American history?

Ask, "If I wanted to know more about the Incas, or the Roman aqueducts, what would I do?" This will tell you how familiar your child has become with resources such as libraries, encyclopedias, and databases.

Ask your child, "How well do you understand the social studies you are learning in school? Is there anything you don't understand? What would you like to know more about?"

6 *Parents and Schools*

As I said in the introduction to this book, parents are critically important to their children's education. By reading to your children daily during the preschool and primary school years, including them in family conversations, listening to them, providing them with varied experiences, and understanding that play and the exploration of diverse objects and environments are vital elements of learning, you can contribute greatly to your children's development and help them become successful learners. And as your children advance through the elementary into the intermediate and middle grades, they continue to need the active interest of their parents. They need to see that their parents care about them and their learning. Furthermore, children should know that their parents value language and are inquisitive about the world—that their parents, in fact, are also learners.

It is crucial for parents to continue reading to their children, sharing interesting stories from the newspapers and magazines as well as from the rich literature of mythology, biography, and travel. They should take walks with their children, making note of the environment and posing interesting questions along the way.

Playing board games that demand problem solving, or watching television and discussing the programs afterward, are also ways to share in a child's learning while fostering a healthy relationship.

As children get older and move through middle school and secondary school, their interactions with their parents necessarily change. But parents' support remains important. Parents will find that taking an interest in what their children are reading and writing is an excellent starting point for conversations, no matter what age the children are. They will also discover that they can learn a great deal from their adolescent children, who may be reading literature or studying historical and scientific topics that the parents either never knew or have forgotten.

The parents' partnership with the school is also important. Maintaining this partnership may seem easier and more natural when children are in the primary grades, but parents should consider it a priority throughout *all* the grades. In the best situations, teachers actively seek connections with parents. They call on the phone, write personal letters, and hold informal discussions. And they make certain that conferences are scheduled for times when parents are able to attend. If teachers do not do these things, then parents should ask *why*.

Parents should expect their children's teachers to explain fully what the school year will be like, what topics will be studied, what problems are to be explored, what is to be read, what kinds of writing will be done, how the teachers will assess their students' progress, and how parents will be kept informed. If this information is not made available to parents, the parents should ask for it regularly.

To make the most of whatever information teachers provide, parents should try to spend some time—a couple of days each year at a minimum—in their child's classroom, especially during the elementary school years. This gives parents valuable direct insight into what their children's educational experiences are like. It also helps them understand the intentions of their children's teachers, which makes interactions between parents and teachers more constructive.

Many teachers actively encourage parents to be classroom partners. Parents may share some of their own experiences, read to children, take small groups of children on field trips, and the like. A few hours each week for such participation is very useful to both parents and their children.

How should parents approach their children's teachers and the schools? In most cases the teacher-parent exchange will be relatively easy. Teachers *want* connections with parents. They understand well the importance of parents as first and ongoing educators of their children. But they also know that parents have not always been sufficiently involved with their children or particularly responsive to teachers' efforts to interact with them. Both parents and teachers must strive for constructive, reciprocal exchanges.

Parents know their children. They know their interests and preferences, how they approach new situations, and how much they understand of the world. Parents need to share this knowledge with teachers in order to help the teachers be more effective. If your son or daughter is unhappy with school, feels unsuccessful or bored, seems not to be making progress as a learner, or is unable to take part in many of the conversations outlined in chapter 5, make an appointment with the child's teacher. *This is an important first step.*

Your meeting with the teacher should not be confrontational or angry. There is no need for defensiveness or anxiety. Share your concerns in as natural a manner as possible. If you have sensed that your child is unhappy about school, the teacher has probably sensed this also. If you have noticed that your child has lost interest in reading, seems uninquisitive about the natural world, or appears vague about mathematics and its uses, the teacher has probably observed these attitudes too. Now is the time for you and the teacher to come together on behalf of the child. Together, parents and teachers can figure out how to proceed. You might ask how you can be more helpful. Can the teacher suggest ways for you to enlarge your child's understanding of math, science, or language? Also inquire about what the teacher will do. Establish a schedule for meeting again to determine what progress is being made, and *keep* the schedule. If you create and maintain a seriousness of purpose where your child's education is concerned, you have taken a vital step toward improving the child's education.

As I said at the beginning, this book is intended to bring parents, children, and teachers together in a productive exchange centered on school learning. Most children, being the natural learners they are, will make academic progress in school—but their progress will be far greater if their parents are actively involved.

The schools generally meet students' needs reasonably well, if not always well enough. But they will also do far better if parents join with teachers in an active partnership. Chapter 1 of this book describes some of the qualities of a healthy school learning environment. An active partnership between parents and schools is necessary if such environments are to become the reality in all schools. Teachers should be supported in their desire for smaller classes in the early years, for a wide range of instructional materials, for strong arts programs. By providing such support, parents benefit their children and all children.

Books Parents Might Find Useful

Armstrong, Thomas. *Awakening Your Child's Natural Genius.* Los Angeles: J. P. Tarcher, 1987.

———. *In Their Own Way: Discovery and Encouraging Your Child's Personal Learning Style.* Los Angeles: J. P. Tarcher, 1987.

Bissex, Glenda. *Gnys at Wrk: A Child Learns to Write and Read.* Cambridge: Harvard University Press, 1980.

Burns, Marilyn. *The I Hate Mathematics! Book.* Boston: Little, Brown, 1975.

Caulkins, Lucy M. *Lessons from a Child.* Portsmouth, NH: Heinemann, 1986.

Children's Television Workshop Parents' Guide to Learning. *Kids Who Love to Learn.* New York: Prentice Hall, 1989.

Clay, Marie. *Writing Begins at Home.* Portsmouth, NH: Heinemann, 1987.

Gardner, Howard. *Frames of Mind: The Theory of Multiple Intelligence.* New York: Basic Books, 1983.

Goodlad, John I. *A Place Called School.* New York: McGraw-Hill, 1987.

Healy, Jane. *Your Child's Growing Mind: A Parent's Guide to Learning from Birth to Adolescence.* New York: Doubleday, 1987.

Kline, Peter. *The Everyday Genius: Restoring Children's Natural Joy of Learning.* Arlington, VA: Great Ocean, 1988.

Lappe, Frances Moore. *What To Do After You Turn Off the TV.* New York: Ballantine, 1985.

Maeroff, Gene. *The School-Smart Parent.* New York: Random House, 1989.

Papert, Seymour. *Mindstorms: Children, Computers, and Powerful Ideas.* New York: Basic Books, 1980.

Rosner, Jerome. *Helping Children Overcome Learning Difficulties.* New York: Walker, 1979.

Schimmels, Cliff. *How To Help Your Child Survive and Thrive in Public Schools.* New York: Revell, 1982.

Schon, Isabel. *Books in Spanish for Children and Young Adults.* Metuchen, NJ: Scarecrow Press, 1985.

Singer, Dorothy, et al. *Use TV to Your Child's Advantage: The Parent's Guide.* Washington, DC: Acropolis, 1990.

Stein, Sara. *The Science Book.* Boston: Little, Brown, 1975.

Taylor, Denny. *Family Literacy: Young Children Learning to Read and Write.* Portsmouth, NH: Heinemann, 1983.

Weitzman, David. *My Backyard History Book.* Boston: Little, Brown, 1975.

Wilms, Denise, and Ilene Cooper. *A Guide to Non-Sexist Children's Books.* Chicago: Academy, 1987.

Several Guides to Good Literature for Elementary School–Age Children

American Library Association. *Opening Doors for Pre-School Children and Their Parents.* Washington, DC: American Library Association, 1981.

Jett-Simpson, May, ed. *Adventuring with Books.* Urbana, IL: National Council of Teachers of English, 1989.

Lamme, Linda. *Growing Up Reading: Sharing With Your Child the Joys of Reading.* Washington, DC: Acropolis, 1985.

Lipson, Eden Ross. *The New York Times Parent's Guide to the Best Books for Children.* New York: Times Books, 1991.

Lorrick, Nancy. *A Parent's Guide to Children's Reading.* New York: Bantam, 1982.

Pollock, Barbara. *The Black Experience in Children's Books.* New York: New York Public Libraries, 1984.

Booklists

Each Spring, *Booklist*, the journal of the American Library Association, publishes a list of notable books for children, based on "literary quality, originality of text and illustrations, design, format, subject matter of interest to children, and likelihood of acceptance by children."

The Fall issue of *The Reading Teacher*, published by the International Reading Association, lists books children themselves select each year as "best books."

The Spring issue of *Social Education*, published by the National Council of the Social Studies, lists books selected each year that "are written primarily for children . . . ; emphasize human relations; present an original theme." (Available at no charge by sending a stamped, self-addressed #10 envelope to the Children's Book Council, 568 Broadway, Suite 404, New York, NY 10012.)

The Spring issue of *Science and Children*, the journal of the National Science Teachers Association, lists children's books selected annually for readability and science accuracy and interest. (Available at no charge by sending a stamped, self-addressed #10 envelope to the Children's Book Council, 568 Broadway, Suite 404, New York, NY 10012.)

VITO PERRONE is Director of Teacher Education and Chair of Teaching, Curriculum, and Learning Environments at Harvard University. He has previous experience as a public school teacher, a university professor of history, education, and peace studies (University of North Dakota), and as dean of the New School and the Center for Teaching and Learning (both at the University of North Dakota). Dr. Perrone has written extensively about such issues as educational equity, humanities curriculum, progressive education, and evaluation. His most recent books are: *A Letter to Teachers: Reflections on Schooling and the Art of Teaching*; *Enlarging Student Assessment in Schools*; *Working Papers: Reflections on Teachers, Schools, and Communities*; *Visions of Peace*; and *Johanna Knudsen Miller: A Pioneer Teacher*.